O9-AIF-472

portion of this book may be reproduced or utilized
electronic, mechanical, or other means, without the
written permission of the publisher.

Printed in Canada
Published by Sasquatch Books
Distributed by PGW/Perseus
12 11 10 09 08   9 8 7 6 5 4 3 2

design by View Design Company

ss Cataloging-in-Publication Data is available.
ISBN-10: 1-57061-557-8
ISBN-13: 978-1-57061-557-3

Sasquatch Books
9 South Main Street, Suite 400
Seattle, WA 98104
(206) 467-4300
www.sasquatchbooks.com
custserv@sasquatchbooks.com

THE

ERIC

C

15 14

Bo

Library of Con

CONTENTS

I CONFIDENTLY *trust that the American people will prove themselves... too wise not to detect the false pride or the dangerous ambitions or the selfish schemes which so often hide themselves under that deceptive cry of mock patriotism: "Our country, right or wrong!" They will not fail to recognize that our dignity, our free institutions and the peace and welfare of this and coming generations of Americans will be secure only as we cling to the watchword of true patriotism: "Our country— when right to be kept right; when wrong to be put right."*

—SENATOR CARL SCHURZ, CHICAGO, ILLINOIS, OCTOBER 17, 1899

A Politics
of Purpose

THE IDEAS CONTAINED IN THIS VOLUME are a consequence of frustration—the frustration that two Americans felt with our nation's political culture at the beginning of the 21st century. We are both the sons of immigrants, and both have benefited enormously from the opportunities that America makes possible. We *are* the American dream and we are immeasurably grateful.

But in recent years, we've become despondent over the way politics plays out in our extraordinary country. We are still sickened at how the moment after September 11 was squandered: a moment when the world was with us, utterly, and when all Americans were yearning to be part of something greater than ourselves. We abhor the way political conversation has, ever since, settled back into a predictable pattern of cheap polarization, staged conflicts and false choices. We reject the idea that politics is about the promotion of one's narrow self-interest, and the underlying myth that millions of little acts of selfishness add up somehow to a healthy community. We believe that in these cynical times—especially in these times—there should be a higher call to country first.

Readers should know that we are progressive and Democrats. But while we are appalled by much of what we hear from the right wing of the Republican Party, we freely admit that conservatives have been correct about certain ideas: the need to tie reward to work, and punishment to crime; the importance of drawing lines between right and wrong; the dangers of a "no consequences" culture.

We also believe that for too long, the Democratic Party has lacked a compelling story that can capture the moral and political imagination of most

Americans. Too many of our progressive friends are content either to carp from the sidelines, to wait for Republican acts of self-destruction, or to play tactical word games that position progressive stances palatably while failing to articulate an overarching vision of the original purposes of politics and policy.

We are particularly frustrated that so much of our politics today consists of lines first written during the clashes, domestic and foreign, of the 1960s. This "Groundhog Day" approach to replaying the culture war's tropes is perhaps nowhere in greater evidence than in how Americans talk about patriotism.

Patriotism, as an idea, has been co-opted over the course of a generation by right-wingers who use the flag not as a symbol of transcendent national unity, but as a sectarian cudgel against the hippies, Francophiles, free-lovers and tree-huggers who constitute their caricature of the American left. The American left, for its part, has been so beaten down by this star-spangled caricature that it has largely ceded the very notion of patriotism to the right. As a result, the first reaction of far too many progressives to any talk of patriotism is automatic, allergic recoil. Needless to say, this reaction simply tightens the screws of the right's imprisoning caricature.

In these pages we offer an alternative.

Both of us operate in our daily lives from the precept that if you don't like something then you must either offer an alternative or shut up. We realized to our dismay that as much as we disliked what others said in politics, we had little better to offer. As dissatisfied as we were with conservative and liberal answers to the question "What do you really believe, and why?", we had no good answer of our own. This document, then, written in the spirit of Thomas Paine's "Common Sense" and the other American pamphlets of the founders' era, is our answer to that self-imposed question.

Our aim was to answer this question in *moral* terms, not to offer a list of issue positions. We believe all politics is fundamentally about morality: What rules do we need to live a good life together? How should those rules govern the choices we make not only as individuals but as a community? The needs that politics must meet are not merely material. A winning and worthy politics—a politics of purpose—should address wants, fears and yearnings that are about the most primordial choices humans make—and it should tip the scales in every choice from selfishness toward social good.

Today, however, progressive politics is replete with leaders who, in the best case, enumerate the policies they like or don't like, while revealing little about their deeper moral choice-making. This lets us know how these leaders might *vote*, but not who they *are*. And while highly engaged and sophisticated voters may be able to "reverse engineer" a moral system from policy positions, the vast majority of voters don't, won't or can't. That's why it is essential that progressive leaders learn anew how to speak in moral terms. Because only by letting us know who they truly are can they earn our lasting support.

We were cheered by the 2006 elections, in which Democrats won and Republicans lost. But we do not kid ourselves: that election was a negative referendum on a failed administration. In order to lead with a true mandate, and to earn enduring and *affirmative* public trust, progressives have to articulate a coherent moral framework that is compelling to most Americans and *within which* policy positions fit.

That is the method of this pamphlet. The reader will notice that this is not a long document. In fact, the essence of it can be contained in just a few pages, the moral code that follows this introduction. It was far harder to distill and succinctly state what we believed than we thought it would be. Getting that down to a page took months. If this surprises you, we encourage you to try it yourself.

Our values and beliefs were not poll-tested, so we do not know if they represent the views of more than two Americans. But an enormous amount of research went into helping us define and characterize our ideas. We immersed ourselves, through readings and interviews, in philosophy, politics, linguistics, religion, demographics and history. We talked to professors, preachers and politicians. We listened to many ordinary Americans. We carefully read and analyzed the writings and speeches of the Americans we admired most and through that tried to understand and connect with the deepest traditions and narrative of American life.

We freely admit that there is not one original idea in this pamphlet. We simply captured the essence of what America's civic leaders and heroes have been saying for over 200 years. It was through our year of research that we realized America doesn't need a *new* politics, it simply needs to reconnect with its *original* patriotic traditions.

Those traditions are grounded in civic virtue, in the simple precept of country above self. They rest on a notion of *public* morality, which is a very different notion of morality than the one that dominates contemporary elections. Ultimately, we seek the revival of a civil religion: a patriotism that every American can be proud of.

Why patriotism as the template for our beliefs? The first reason is visceral: we simply love this country. We want to make it safer for other people to say that—and we want to make it harder too. No one should feel sheepish about professing patriotism, but no one should be able to get away with mere professions. Patriotism may begin in reflex but it must lead to reflection—and result in action. This pamphlet is designed to provoke both reflection and action about an idea we too often fail to take seriously.

We aren't neutral. As we said, we are active progressive citizens. We hold many liberal beliefs. But we aren't blind either. Today only one in five voters self-identifies as "liberal." Yet a deeper probe into the values of voters reveals that a great majority would embrace the patriotic virtues we lay out in this document—virtues, as you will see, that we believe to be *inherently* progressive. In short, we think our particular conception of patriotism can bring people back into the progressive fold and create a lasting electoral majority.

The final reason for patriotism as our frame is strategic. In American life, the idea of freedom reigns nearly supreme. To be more precise, a negative conception of freedom—the right to be let alone and to make choices without regard to others—dominates law, politics and culture. Within limits, we appreciate such freedom. At the same time, we despair at how this negative kind of freedom talk—*I should be able to do what I please*—can be used to justify base selfishness. We came to see, as we wrestled with this, that the only thing in America that trumps freedom talk is patriotism: an appeal not to self-oriented choice but to shared pride in what our freedom has enabled, pride in being part of a world-changing experiment.

In recent months, "the common good" has emerged as another conceptual frame for progressives. We love talk of the common good. It arises from exactly the same set of principles we believe in, and it reminds us that rugged individualism is no way to get a barn built. But while common-good rhetoric is necessary, it is not sufficient. We just don't think it packs the same punch as patriotism. Pound for pound, an appeal to pride is more powerful than the idea of sharing. We want to take that fact of human nature and exploit it—for the common good.

We are keenly aware that our brand of patriotism will make certain people uncomfortable. Some on the right may bristle at our contention that American patriotism is inherently progressive. But it is: this country was invented in the name of progress, justice, and betterment of self and society. Some on the left may fear that patriotism is by definition xenophobic. But it isn't: the American experiment is special precisely because we amalgamate the peoples and ideas of the world. Love of country has, no doubt, been invoked to justify many acts of barbarism in human history. But love of *this* country—an embrace of what America *ideally* embodies—means love of universal ideals of human rights and aspiration.

Finally, there will be those across the political spectrum who assert that we now live in a post-national world where threats and opportunities transcend borders and where patriotism has no place. But that's misguided. Even though national borders are less meaningful today than they once were, nation-states are still the dominant agents of change, for good or ill. And again, it is especially in a globalizing age that America matters uniquely—ours is the only nation designed to mesh cultures together and create new, heartier hybrids. No place better embodies, and no nation has more leverage to propagate, the very qualities of an enlightened global community.

Whether we do so, of course, depends on who gets to wield the levers of national power in America and how well-grounded those men and women will be in the origins of their own beliefs. This pamphlet is intended to influence both those variables.

So—enough of the preliminaries. In this volume you will find several pieces of work, organized as variations on a theme. We begin with a simple moral code: a distillation of what we believe to be true patriotism. That is followed by a manifesto that puts the code in context, describing the situation we Americans find ourselves in today, and offering our alternative, a proudly progressive conception of patriotism that all Americans can embrace. Then comes what we call a "Ten-Principle Plan," illustrating the public policy choices that flow from our core values—but, crucially, emphasizing that leaders should lead *first* with deep principle rather than specific points of policy. Following that, we've written a model speech that we would give and that we invite others to use or adapt to spark debate about patriotism and public morality. Finally, we close with a set of challenges and questions for you, the reader.

We've included, every few pages, excerpts from foundational American texts and speeches. We treasure them. As you come upon the words of John Winthrop, Washington and Jefferson, Abraham Lincoln, Susan B. Anthony, the Roosevelts, the Kennedys, King, and others, the chords of connection between our times and theirs become more visible. In the same spirit, we've included a visual essay of iconic American images, some very familiar and others less so, all part of the palimpsest of patriotism.

The values and ideas articulated in these pages represent what we believe when we say "true patriot." What do *you* believe?

Eric Liu and Nick Hanauer
Seattle, Washington, May 2007
truepat.org

Declaration of Independence

WE hold these truths to be self-evident, that all men are created equal, that they are endowed by their Creator with certain unalienable Rights, that among these are Life, Liberty and the pursuit of Happiness. — That to secure these rights, Governments are instituted among Men, deriving their just powers from the consent of the governed, — That whenever any Form of Government becomes destructive of these ends, it is the Right of the People to alter or to abolish it, and to institute new Government, laying its foundation on such principles and organizing its powers in such form, as to them shall seem most likely to effect their Safety and Happiness.

————

ABRAHAM LINCOLN

The Gettysburg Address

Four score and seven years ago our fathers brought forth on this continent a new nation, conceived in Liberty, and dedicated to the proposition that all men are created equal.

Now we are engaged in a great civil war, testing whether that nation, or any nation so conceived and so dedicated, can long endure. We are met on a great battle-field of that war. We have come to dedicate a portion of that field as a final resting-place for those who here gave their lives that that nation might live. It is altogether fitting and proper that we should do this.

But, in a larger sense, we can not dedicate—we can not consecrate—we can not hallow—this ground. The brave men, living and dead, who struggled here, have consecrated it far above our poor power to add or detract. The world will little note nor long remember what we say here, but it can never forget what they did here. It is for us, the living, rather, to be dedicated here to the unfinished work which they who fought here have thus far so nobly advanced. It is rather for us to be here dedicated to the great task remaining before us—that from these honored dead we take increased devotion to that cause for which they gave the last full measure of devotion—that we here highly resolve that these dead shall not have died in vain—that this nation, under God, shall have a new birth of freedom—and that government of the people, by the people, for the people, shall not perish from the earth.

The Patriot's
Moral Code

WE ARE PATRIOTS. We believe in the greatness of America's national ideals. We believe America has an indispensable purpose in the world: to demonstrate, by example, the power of freedom and equal opportunity.

True patriots know that America was founded in freedom—freedom to speak, to worship, to choose whatever path to happiness suits us best—but that with freedom comes an equal responsibility to country, community and family.

True patriots believe that what enables a free society to remain strong is a set of traditional virtues and values: pragmatism tied to principle, honesty and integrity, hard work and personal initiative, responsibility and self-discipline, fairness and compassion, competitive striving and fair play, a desire to serve the nation and a kinship with the world.

True patriots believe that freedom from responsibility is selfishness, freedom from sacrifice is cowardice, freedom from tolerance is prejudice, freedom from stewardship is exploitation, and freedom from compassion is cruelty.

True patriots know that we should measure our nation's progress by whether *every* citizen has a fair shot to advance on the basis of talent and merit, and by the degree to which we promote the common success of *all* our citizens. Freedom without an equal chance to enjoy it is no freedom at all.

True patriots believe it is immoral when inequality of *opportunity* leads to and perpetuates inequality *itself.* On a truly level playing field, some will do much better than others because we are not all equally talented or motivated. But when the tilt of the field keeps even the talented from ever winning, that is unfair and un-American.

True patriots believe that we should measure a citizen's worth by contribution to country and community, not by wealth or power—that those whom America has benefited most should contribute in proportion to their good fortune—and that serving others should be esteemed more highly than serving self.

These were the ideals of the founders of our country and the defenders of our union. They have made America unique and necessary from the beginning. And now it is time for them to inspire a new generation of Americans.

———

GEORGE WASHINGTON

FROM HIS

Farewell Address

September 19, 1796

CITIZENS by birth or choice of a common country, that country has a right to concentrate your affections.—The name of AMERICAN, which belongs to you, in your national capacity, must always exalt the just pride of Patriotism, more than any appellation derived from local discriminations. With slight shades of difference, you have the same Religion, Manners, Habits, and Political Principles. You have in a common cause fought and triumphed together; the Independence and Liberty you possess are the work of joint counsels, and joint efforts—of common dangers, sufferings, and successes.

First Inaugural Address

March 4, 1801

LET us, then, fellow-citizens, unite with one heart and one mind. Let us restore to social intercourse that harmony and affection without which liberty and even life itself are but dreary things. And let us reflect that, having banished from our land that religious intolerance under which mankind so long bled and suffered, we have yet gained little if we countenance a political intolerance as despotic, as wicked, and capable of as bitter and bloody persecutions.

Dedication of the
Bunker Hill Monument

June 17, 1825

AND let the sacred obligations which have devolved on this generation and on us sink deep into our hearts. Those are daily dropping from among us who established our liberty and our government. The great trust now descends to new hands. Let us apply ourselves to that which is presented to us as our appropriate object. We can win no laurels in a war for independence. Earlier and worthier hands have gathered them all. Nor are there places for us by the side of Solon, and Alfred, and other founders of states. Our fathers have filled them. But there remains to us a great duty of defense and preservation; and there is opened to us also a noble pursuit to which the spirit of the times strongly invites us.

Our proper business is improvement. Let our age be the age of improvement. In a day of peace let us advance the arts of peace and the works of peace. Let us develop the resources of our land, call forth its powers, build up its institutions, promote all its great interests, and see whether we also, in our day and generation, may not perform something worthy to be remembered. Let us cultivate a true spirit of union and harmony. In pursuing the great objects which our condition points out to us, let us act under a settled conviction, and a habitual feeling that these twenty-four states are one country. Let our conceptions be enlarged to the circle of our duties. Let us extend our ideas over the whole of the vast field in which we are called to act. Let our object be our country, our whole country, and nothing but our country. And by the blessing of God may that country itself become a vast and splendid monument, not of oppression and terror, but of wisdom, of peace, and of liberty, upon which the world may gaze with admiration forever.

FRANKLIN DELANO ROOSEVELT

FROM HIS

State of the Union Address

January 6, 1941

For there is nothing mysterious about the foundations of a healthy and strong democracy. The basic things expected by our people of their political and economic systems are simple. They are:

Equality of opportunity for youth and for others.

Jobs for those who can work.

Security for those who need it.

The defending of those who need it.

The preservation of civil liberties for all.

The enjoyment of the fruits of scientific progress in a wider and constantly rising standard of living.

These are the simple, basic things that must never be lost sight of in the turmoil and unbelievable complexity of our modern world. The inner and abiding strength of our economic and political systems is dependent upon the degree to which they fulfill these expectation.

In the future days, which we seek to make secure, we look forward to a world founded upon four essential human freedoms.

The first is freedom of speech and expressions—everywhere in the world.

The second is freedom of every person to worship God in his own way—everywhere in the world.

The third is freedom from want—which, translated into world terms, means economic understandings which will secure to every nation a healthy peacetime life for its inhabitants—everywhere in the world.

The fourth is freedom from fear—which, translated into world terms, means a world-wide reduction of armaments to such a point and in such a thorough fashion that no nation will be in a position to commit an act of physical aggression against any neighbor—anywhere in the world.

True Patriotism
A Manifesto

NO NATION ON EARTH has America's greatness of spirit and purpose.

There are other great nations, to be sure: great in scale or power. *But no other nation on earth is dedicated to a proposition.* No other nation was founded to give people a second chance. No other nation prides itself on being the world's laboratory, demonstrating what happens when you intermingle the peoples of the earth.

Across the span of centuries, America has embodied the very essence of human striving: we have set forth great ideals and have tried to live by them. We have sometimes faltered, sometimes failed. We have always tried again. With each generation, we inch closer to fulfilling our promise. Ever perfectible but never perfect, America is in a constant state of becoming, and this unending progress is our heritage.

But America today is in danger of drifting from its best traditions. We have allowed false prophets of selfishness to obscure our vision. We have grown numb to a creeping cynicism about progress and public life. We crave human connection yet hide behind walls. We worship the money chase yet decry the toll it exacts on us. We allow the market to dominate our lives, relationships, yearnings and aspirations. We indulge in nostalgia and irony and addictive entertainment, then purge from our hearts any true idealism or passion, any notion that being American should mean something more than "everyday low prices" or "every man for himself."

In the midst of this dislocation and disorientation, so many Americans today yearn for higher purpose, for calling—for some assurance that life matters. We wish to believe there is more to our days than is revealed on our screens. Make no mistake: this is a spiritual crisis. And many of us have found spiritual salves in houses of worship. But we are in a social and political crisis as well. And the time has come for a new great awakening, a revival of the creed and the covenant of our civil religion. The time has come to replenish the content of American character and the meaning of American life.

It is time to return to true patriotism.

What does it mean today to be patriotic? Patriotism means pride. But true patriotism is *earned* pride: It means appreciating not only what is great about our country but also *what it takes* to create and sustain greatness. It means being proud of how we treat each other, how we plan for the future, how we meet challenges and threats. True patriotism celebrates the hard choices needed to create more opportunity for more people, and the values that guide those choices.

Unfortunately, in too many quarters patriotism is understood to celebrate might for its own sake, power as its own end. Patriotism has become a cheap brand, a soundtrack and package of graphics signaling complacent conformity: wave your flag, but don't rock the boat. Patriotism, to many Americans, signifies only empty swagger. It has been wrested by self-satisfied salesmen singing, "You're with us or against us." It has been used to justify dubious acts of war-making and lawmaking. It has been stolen to silence dissent.

This crime has a perpetrator and an accomplice. The far right has stolen and perverted the idea of patriotism. It has used the flag shamelessly as sword and shield in its narrow partisan campaign for advantage. But the far left is culpable as well: of an intolerable passivity, an acquiescence to this brazen theft of patriotism itself. The more the right uses the flag to proclaim its toughness, to belittle the defenders of the weak, to celebrate winners, the more the left shrinks from the flag—and in so doing, ratifies the right's illegitimate claims.

But try as they might in this time of war to make patriotism theirs in perpetuity, the jingoists cannot deny what the people know. We, the people, know: that there is more to patriotism than the beating of chests; that he who professes too loudly how strong and unbeatable he is, protests too much; that dissent is as much a measure of patriotism as service is. And our knowledge will prevail.

We, the people, believe it is time for progressives to reclaim patriotism—not to reinvent it but to restore it; to return to a tradition that is more than chauvinism or showboating. It is time to rededicate ourselves to a true American patriotism, a civil religion of purpose that answers our deepest needs and fears in this time of uncertainty. And this patriotism belongs not to party but to country.

It is time to distinguish, with brutal honesty, between false patriots and true American patriots.

False patriots think that wearing little flags on their lapels is the full measure of their patriotic duty. True patriots may sometimes wear such flags too but know that acts, not badges, are the true marker of devotion to country.

False patriots say that liberty means simply being let alone. True patriots know that liberty is not just the removal of tyranny or encumbrance; it is the cultivation of a freedom worth having—and this requires common endeavor and shared sacrifice.

False patriots say that the pursuit of happiness means getting as much for yourself as you can; that accumulating wealth is righteous. True patriots know that the real American Dream is to build a legacy that endures; to aspire for your children more than for yourself, and to leave them with truly equal opportunities to live to the fullest of their potential.

False patriots say that diversity and dissent threaten our cohesiveness and comfort our enemies. True patriots know that what frightens our enemies, foreign and domestic, is our capacity for diversity, disagreement and synthesis.

False patriots think that ideology—*their* ideology—is the only pure way, and they champion ideology over the facts of science or common sense. True patriots know that such fundamentalism is fundamentally un-American—and that the strongest streak in the American character is a fierce pragmatism that mistrusts blind ideology of every stripe and insists on finding what really *works*.

False patriots say that we're number one because

we're the biggest, the richest and the mightiest. True patriots know that America is number one because of our ethos of hard work, fair play and second chances—and that if we are to remain the world's beacon, we must remain faithful to those values and set a powerful example.

False patriots say that the wealth of the wealthy is proof of their virtue. True patriots know that until we have a level playing field, on which talent can compete fairly against talent, risk can be shared more fairly, and virtue can emerge without regard to inherited benefits and burdens—until this day comes, having money means only having money.

False patriots treat the land, air and water as their personal dominion, to exploit as they please. True patriots know that we are but stewards, and that our obligation to God and posterity should limit our temptations to exploit.

False patriots say they love America but hate the government. True patriots know that government is the physical manifestation of teamwork and mutual obligation in any free, democratic society.

False patriots say that taxes take away the hard-earned money of self-made men. True patriots know that there is no such thing as a self-made man—that every fortune was built upon safe roads, strong backs, clean air, and bright minds developed by the community, through taxes—and that taxes are therefore not just the price we pay for a healthy nation but the gift we make to our own children.

True American patriotism means freedom, *with responsibility.*

Opportunity, with personal initiative.

Purpose, through sacrifice and service.

Community above self.

Contribution over consumption.

Stewardship, not exploitation.

Leadership by example.

Pragmatism tied to principle.

A fair shot for all.

These principles form the core of true patriotism. They are pro-progress, pro-truth, pro-trust, pro-fairness, pro-security and pro-peace. They are, if anything, the distilled precepts of every great faith tradition in American life. They are the commandments of our American civic religion. These principles reveal to us that our best life is not to be purchased on credit, ordered on demand, or reaped in a windfall. True American patriotism calls us to be more than what we are now: to be independent in thought; to be tougher, on ourselves first; to be more compassionate, toward strangers as well as family; to hold fast to old-fashioned ideas of honor even when doing so makes us seem naive; and to judge others sternly— but according to their adherence to this code, not by the badges of their status or station.

What we have stated here is a *public* morality. For too long in our politics, morality has been defined as a set of narrow bedroom issues. These issues are real and often raise wrenching private choices. But of far more consequence to the nation is the morality of our public lives, our public choices and our public actions.

At the heart of our public morality is the idea that he who gives generously is most virtuous and morally praiseworthy; that there is no greater citizen than she who sacrifices; and that there is no greater measure of worth than contribution. These are values we can be proud of. After all, there is no moral system or religion on earth where the guiding ethic is "grab more for yourself."

Today, however, sacrifice is not shared at all equally. Millions of Americans are working harder than ever, raising the GNP and pumping up productivity—and yet their own wages remain stagnant and their safety net ragged. These Americans are one missed payment away from foreclosure; one ailment away from financial disaster. Tens of thousands of other Americans are risking life and limb in wars around the world. The current administration has failed utterly to meet these challenges.

The problem, though, extends beyond an abysmal administration that, eventually, shall pass. Today's leaders—in both parties—fail to challenge us to raise our sights. They do not ask those who have received most to give back in like measure. They do not ask those in the broad middle class to do much more than keep on shopping, or to imagine a vision of citizenship beyond mere consumption. They do not ask us to serve in places where all citizens—rich or poor, of whatever color—are, for a time, equal. They do not honor us that way. They pander. They promise easy solutions with no sacrifice. They prefer, instead, to enshrine selfishness and self-indulgence—and they pretend that patriotism is just self-love writ large.

But to love our country truly means to rise above "I am because I am." It is to recognize that "I am because *we are.*" Love of country cannot be a super-sized version of individual narcissism. True love of country—of this country—is love of our children, of a creed that promises *them* a better life before it promises us anything, and embraces the sacrifices needed to make that better life. True love of country is giving ourselves to a cause and a purpose larger than ourselves. And that cause is to make liberty worth having, to make the pursuit of happiness deeper than the quest for personal pleasure, and to leave a legacy of progress and possibility.

We will concede that the tenets of true American patriotism are idealistic—in exactly the way that Thomas Paine was when he penned "Common

Sense," or when Thomas Jefferson wrote the Declaration of Independence. Or when Abraham Lincoln spoke of a union that could not, would not, falter. In exactly the way that Theodore Roosevelt demanded that the state protect the public against the concentration of monopolistic wealth. In exactly the way that Franklin Roosevelt knew that freedom from want and disease is bound inextricably to the procedural freedoms of the Bill of Rights.

Progressive patriotism is our program. Pragmatic idealism is our method. Idealism is not ideology: it is belief in the possibility of progress. It is faith in the next American Dream. And it is a faith that sits perfectly well beside pragmatism, for the things we dream of will be made real only by practical action, by a relentless focus on what truly works rather than on reality-denying doctrine or dogma.

And what, really, is the alternative? We can go on for years or even decades living as we do now, going into debt to pay off debts. We can keep pressing the dispenser button for more morphine-like distraction and amusement to numb us. We can keep on plundering the present without regard to the future.

We can keep adding layers of makeup on our ugly made-for-TV politics. We can continue allowing a few elites to rig the game in their favor. We can keep worshipping the market and keep imagining ourselves not as citizens but as consumers.

But why should we?

Instead, we can return to the practical way of being an American that every generation has known: a way of being that dispenses with fantasy and with orthodoxy and every other form of self-delusion. A way of being that looks squarely at the challenge and asks "What will it take for us to fulfill our promise?" The American way is always to be searching for a better way; to question constantly whether we are living up to our ideals and whether ideology is distorting our vision. At the heart of this is a commitment to a process: a faith that in a land of so many factions, relentlessly fair and pragmatic inquiry will bring us closer to truth.

It is time to face the ailments of our society, reckon with the wounds—and see then that to be American still means something great. Greatness lies not in the impermanent things like fame and power and material abundance. It lies in the integrity of our choices, the veneration of traditional values, the assumption of responsibility and the welcoming of sacrifice. Greatness is found in a society where fair play is not a slogan for fools but is the covenant that binds us together. It is found in the decision to serve someone else before oneself. It is found in the courage to face painful truths about the true costs of our actions and omissions. It is found in the fortitude to defer the many gratifications all around us. It is found in the power to triumph over lethargy and drift. It must be earned, continuously.

Greatness resides in leaders who ask us to be more than what we have been so far. Truly patriotic political leaders do not ask first about party or electoral prospects; they ask first about country. They ask us to do more. They tell us things we may not want to hear, but should.

At this moment, such leaders are few and far between. But ultimately, and blessedly, greatness resides in the heart of every American, for each of us is the heir to a tradition that far outshines the current culture of corruption and disengagement. So it is time now for us all to declare and sustain a new American patriotism: to call out that greatness within each of us, to challenge each other to choose as the first Americans did—with the next generation in mind—and to dream like the best Americans always have—with the next century in mind. It is time to weave our national life back into the tapestry of virtue that made America's past glorious and that can make our future more glorious still.

This is the promise of a new American patriotism. It is a promise we must all keep.

THEODORE ROOSEVELT

FROM

The New Nationalism

Osawatomie, Kansas, August 31, 1910

IN every wise struggle for human betterment one of the main objects, and often the only object, has been to achieve in large measure equality of opportunity. In the struggle for this great end, nations rise from barbarism to civilization, and through it people press forward from one stage of enlightenment to the next. One of the chief factors in progress is the destruction of special privilege. The essence of any struggle for healthy liberty has always been, and must always be, to take from some one man or class of men the right to enjoy power, or wealth, or position, or immunity, which has not been earned by service to his or their fellows. That is what you fought for in the Civil War, and that is what we strive for now.

Practical equality of opportunity for all citizens, when we achieve it, will have two great results. First, every man will have a fair chance to make of himself all that in him lies; to reach the highest point to which his capacities, unassisted by special privilege of his own and unhampered by the special privilege of others, can carry him, and to get for himself and his family substantially what he has earned. Second, equality of opportunity means that the commonwealth will get from every citizen the highest service of which he is capable. No man who carries the burden of the special privileges of another can give to the commonwealth that service to which it is fairly entitled. I stand for the square deal. But when I say that I am for the square deal, I mean not merely that I stand for fair play under the present rules of the games, but that I stand for having those rules changed so as to work for a more substantial equality of opportunity and of reward for equally good service.

Recapturing America's Moral Vision

University of Kansas, March 18, 1968

[E]ven if we act to erase material poverty, there is another great task. It is to confront the poverty of satisfaction—a lack of purpose and dignity—that inflicts us all. Too much and too long, we seem to have surrendered community excellence and community values in the mere accumulation of material things. Our gross national product, now, is over eight hundred billion dollars a year, but that GNP—if we should judge America by that—counts air pollution and cigarette advertising, and ambulances to clear our highways of carnage. It counts special locks for our doors and the jails for those who break them. It counts the destruction of our redwoods and the loss of our natural wonder in chaotic sprawl. It counts napalm and the cost of a nuclear warhead, and armored cars for police who fight riots in our streets. It counts Whitman's rifle and Speck's knife, and the television programs which glorify violence in order to sell toys to our children.

Yet the gross national product does not allow for the health of our children, the quality of their education, or the joy of their play. It does not include the beauty of our poetry or the strength of our marriages; the intelligence of our public debate or the integrity of our public officials. It measures neither our wit nor our courage; neither our wisdom nor our learning; neither our compassion nor our devotion to our country; it measures everything, in short, except that which makes life worthwhile. And it can tell us everything about America except why we are proud that we are Americans.

JOHN WINTHROP

FROM

A Model of Christian Charity

1630

FOR this end, we must be knit together in this work as one man. We must entertain each other in brotherly affection. We must be willing to abridge our selves of our superfluities, for the supply of others' necessities. We must uphold a familiar commerce together in all meekness, gentleness, patience, and liberality. We must delight in each other, make others' conditions our own—rejoice together, mourn together, labor and suffer together, always having before our eyes our commission and community in the work, our community as members of the same body. So shall we *keep the unity of the spirit in the bond of peace....*

For we must consider that we shall be as a City upon a Hill. The eyes of all people are upon us; so that if we shall deal falsely with our God in this work we have undertaken and so cause Him to withdraw His present help from us, we shall be made a story and a byword through the world.

Betsy Ross Flag 1777

Flag of 20 stars and 15 stripes 1818

FIFTEEN STARS AND STRIPES

IN CONGRESS. JULY 4, 1776.

The unanimous Declaration of the thirteen united States of America.

Patriotic Values
and Policies

A Ten-Principle Plan

WE CALL THIS SECTION a "ten-principle plan" for a reason. Too often, politicians offer up ten-point plans that are lists of policy positions on various issues rather than enunciations of core values. We believe that policy flows from principles, which are rooted in values. So in our view, any meaningful discussion of policy should begin with—and be organized around—principles. Only when progressives can successfully articulate such a coherent moral framework, *within* which policies fit, will we be able to build an enduring legacy of leadership that most Americans can support and be proud of.

That is how we've approached this section. The policies we discuss here are not the result of some tactical triangulation or split-the-difference moderation. Rather, they are the logical and inevitable consequence of the patriotic principles we state below.

We want to emphasize that we are talking about public morality, not private. We believe far too much attention in American politics has been devoted to the private question of sexual behavior. We are both pro-choice. We happen to believe that gay couples who seek to wed can strengthen the institution of marriage. And we decline to make such private issues the centerpiece of our notion of morality. Indeed, we refuse to discuss them at all. Of far greater consequence, in our view, are the moral consequences of public behavior and public choices.

Last of all, we note that our conception of patriotism requires an active role for government. When citizens come together to solve shared problems, *that is* government, and no functioning society can avoid it. When large numbers of citizens come together to solve large problems, the government that results can become large and bureaucratic.

Government therefore has to be managed well and wisely—but it shouldn't be hated. To hate government is immoral and impractical—because a society with stunted or no government is anarchic, unfair, unequal and ultimately unfree. Government cannot solve everything: as citizens, parents, mentors and volunteers we all share responsibility. But we believe that a true love of America requires a faith that government—citizens pooling resources and working together for the common good—can be part of the solution.

With that, here are some examples of how our patriotic principles play out in public policy:

1) *AMERICAN EXCEPTIONALISM.* America is exceptional. This is not boasting or jingoism; it is fact. We are exceptional in our provenance, founded as we are on universal ideals of freedom and equal opportunity. We are exceptional in our promise, striving as we do still to live up to those ideals. Our purpose in the world is simple: to kindle the flame of a freedom *worth having.* And the world knows this. For all our failings, America has been the object of more hopes and dreams of more people from more places than

any country in human history. But the question is this: *How can we be worthy of such hopes?* We believe America must be unafraid to lead in the world—and unafraid to lead with humility. Humility is hard work. We must lead by example and skillful statecraft, not merely force of arms and bluster. We must get our own fiscal house in order. We must be honest about our errors. We must study the cultures and languages of other countries. We must capitalize upon our diversity at home and cultivate allies abroad. We must learn, in short, how to win friends and influence people: not because we are weak but because we are strong, and because how we carry our might—rather than the might itself—is the true measure of our greatness. Of course, true patriots also recognize the limits of persuasion and "soft power." America has enemies who want to kill Americans. America has adversaries who want to see America weakened. There exist mortal threats and hard moral choices that can make war necessary and just. All the more why wisdom matters. The United States needs to exit the unnecessary war in Iraq responsibly, so that we can replenish our ability to fight the right fights when the time truly comes—

and so that we can restore the luster of our promise and purpose in the world.

2) RESPONSIBILITY FOR THE COMMON GOOD. The hallmark of a healthy society is that those who can carry the heaviest loads, do—and are proud to do it. Those who have benefited most from a multigenerational legacy of sacrifice and public benefits should be most willing and proudest to contribute to the common good. True patriots measure themselves not by personal wealth or power but by the degree to which they contribute to the community. One clear instance of how this principle plays out is tax policy. We believe it is time to state anew—and assertively—the moral case for progressive taxation, restoring the estate tax, and taxing the income from capital and work equally. But more than that: we want to shift the culture so that Americans appreciate the purpose of taxes and can feel prouder to pay them, and so that the wealthiest abandon shameful stratagems to evade taxes altogether. We also believe that those who already do sacrifice—working mothers, for instance—should be supported and rewarded for the ways they strive for the good of others. It is long past time that this nation had paid family and parental leave, and a real child care system that lightens the load mothers carry.

3) EQUALITY OF OPPORTUNITY. The existence of opportunity makes America strong and free but that opportunity has to be available to all, and not concentrated in the hands of a few, in order for it to be truly meaningful. Freedom without equality of opportunity is false freedom. But today the gap between the richest 10 percent and everyone else is wider than it was on the eve of the Great Depression. As the new economy confers compounded advantage to wealthier Americans, and as the middle class takes on more debt just to keep from falling farther behind, the implied promise of a fair shot is fraying. Too many people are inheriting disadvantage. We need economic strategies that will help working Americans accumulate assets and skills. And now more than ever, education is the key to equality of opportunity and the key to America's competitiveness in the world. We believe that a radical reform of our schools, coupled with dramatically higher investment in education—from early learning and

K–12 to higher education and worker retraining—is the most lasting and powerful way to ensure a fair shot for all Americans.

4) PATRIOTIC CAPITALISM. We fervently believe in capitalism and the freedom that makes it possible. We also believe that capitalism is not an end in itself but rather a tool for the nation—and that it is proper for the nation to create rules, boundaries and incentives to harness economic power to national goals. Markets are man-made constructs that benefit some and not others. Patriotic capitalism means having the courage to examine our market constructs continually *and change them* if they are not serving the greater good and our shared national aspirations. Too often in America we equate lower prices with the common good. But America should stand for more than just unbounded consumption. Patriotic capitalists balance short-term economic gain against long-term national priorities. For instance, we believe in the need for energy independence and believe the national government should tax gasoline consumption far more than it does today and that it should promote the development and use of alternative energy far more than it does today. And while we cherish the power of the market to justly reward hard work, talent, discipline and initiative, we also recognize that an unfettered market can unjustly perpetuate or deepen original inequities of opportunity. Truly patriotic business leaders embrace an obligation to help level the economic playing field for all Americans, especially those dislocated by globalizing markets. National economic policy tools should be used to encourage American companies to invest in the American workforce.

5) MUTUAL OBLIGATION. What do we owe one another? In a thriving society, people are willing, to a reasonable degree, to take care of others—and to expect that they would be taken care of in a similar way. The Golden Rule is the moral core of true patriotism. A society cannot remain strong or democratic when those who think they no longer require help can simply opt out of any obligation to help others. We must share risks instead of sloughing them off on those least able to bear them. And we must treat another person's peril, misfortune or vulnerability as something that affects us. This means, for instance, that providing basic health care is an essential responsibility we have for one another. A society in which some people get basic health care and some don't, based on their ability to pay, makes as little sense to us as a society where some get fire protection and some don't. True patriots take care of their own by pooling resources and risk profiles to ensure that no American is denied the minimum of health care needed to be a productive citizen. This is not the red herring of "socialized medicine"—we are committed to a role for the market in the delivery of health care. But that role is servant, not master. The duty we all share—providers, patients, taxpayers—is to sustain a healthy body politic.

6) Service to country. Our patriotic conception of citizenship requires that all Americans, regardless of differences in wealth, status or talent, be equally obligated to serve our nation. The moral value of shared sacrifice is what animates the very idea of citizenship. At one time the draft embodied this value of shared sacrifice. Now more than ever, we believe there is a need to revive it, through a universal national service initiative that can be fulfilled by joining the military, AmeriCorps or civic and community organizations for a defined period of time.

7) STEWARDSHIP. Our notion of patriotism demands that Americans be good stewards of our national treasure in all its forms: our extraordinary natural resources, our infrastructure, our nation's bank account and our people. Our commitment should be to leave our environment in better shape than when we found it, our nation's fiscal house in better order, our public infrastructure in better repair, and our people better educated and healthier. To indulge in immediate gratification and exploitation is an insult to previous generations, who sacrificed for us, and thievery from the next generation, who depend on our virtue. To run a long-term deficit and a continuously unbalanced budget is shameful. It is not how we want to conduct our personal life; it should not be how we conduct our national life.

8) COMMON SENSE VIRTUE. While we believe that in a free society adults should be able to buy, do, watch and wear what they please, it should still be the obligation of our community to promote virtue for our children. This is about common-sense parenting, not politics. It is common sense to want to have less violence and sex pushed at our children, and less junk food in our schools. It is common sense to seek a respite from the relentless social message that people are consumers first and last. And it is common sense to want to raise children who see that buying more stuff is not the path to purpose. We favor polices that help curb the culture of trash and that promote a public-spiritedness that transcends conspicuous consumption.

9) TOLERANCE AND COMMON CAUSE. In this diverse society held together not by blood but by an idea, we have to be tolerant of each other and our differences. More than that, we should encourage newcomers with talent and energy, and move past a punitive and divisive approach to immigration reform. At the same time, for this society actually to achieve its full potential and to leverage its full competitive advantage in the world, we need to make citizenship matter. We need to move beyond mere tolerance to joint *action*. The thing to celebrate is not diversity per se, but what we *do* with diversity. We support public policies that make us make something useful out of our differences. Public education, national service and other shared civic experiences matter because they enable diverse Americans to work side by side, step into each other's shoes, develop a capacity for empathy, and create a deeper basis for common national identity. *E pluribus unum.*

10) PRAGMATISM. We believe that every one of these principles we have enumerated is not just good but practical. And we believe in fact that pragmatism—a relentless focus on what works—is itself a moral principle that is part of the true American way. We stand against ideological orthodoxy, political extremism, partisan point-scoring. These ways of approaching public problems fail because in the end they are not about finding solutions. We believe the value of an idea comes from the fruits it yields for society. We think solutions can come from across the political spectrum, and it is a moral imperative to return our politics to pragmatic, independent thinking about what works for *all* Americans.

FROM

The Strenuous Life

April 10, 1899

I WISH to preach, not the doctrine of ignoble ease, but the doctrine of the strenuous life. The life of toil and effort, of labor and strife; to preach that highest form of success which comes, not to the man who desires mere easy peace, but to the man who does not shrink from danger, from hardship or from bitter toil, and who out of these wins the splendid ultimate triumph.

A life of slothful ease, a life of that peace which springs merely from lack either of desire or of power to strive after great things, is as little worthy of a nation as of an individual. I ask only that what every self-respecting American demands from himself and from his sons shall be demanded of the American nation as a whole....

No country can long endure if its foundations are not laid deep in the material prosperity which comes from thrift, from business energy and enterprise, from hard, unsparing effort in the fields of industrial activity; but neither was any nation ever yet truly great if it relied upon material prosperity alone. All honor must be paid to the architects of our material prosperity, to the great captains of industry who have built our factories and our railroads, to the strong men who toil for wealth with brain or hand; for great is the debt of the nation to these and their kind. But our debt is yet greater to the men whose highest type is to be found in a statesman like Lincoln, a soldier like Grant. They showed by their lives that they recognized the law of work, the law of strife, they toiled to win a competence for themselves and those dependent upon them; but they recognized that there were yet other and even loftier duties—duties to the nation and duties to the race.

I preach to you, then, my countrymen, that our country calls not for the life of ease but for the life of strenuous endeavor. The twentieth century looms before us big with the fate of many nations. If we stand idly by, if we seek merely swollen, slothful ease and ignoble peace, if we shrink from the hard contests where men must win at hazard of their lives and at the risk of all they hold dear, then the bolder and stronger peoples will pass us by, and will win for themselves the domination of the world. Let us therefore boldly face the life of strife, resolute to do our duty well and manfully; resolute to uphold righteousness by deed and by word; resolute to be both honest and brave, to serve high ideals, yet to use practical methods. Above all, let us shrink from no strife, moral or physical, within or without the nation, provided we are certain that the strife is justified, for it is only through strife, through hard and dangerous endeavor, that we shall ultimately win the goal of true national greatness.

Address at "I Am an American" Day, Central Park, New York"

May 21, 1944

AND what is this liberty which must lie in the hearts of men and women? It is not the ruthless, the unbridled will; it is not freedom to do as one likes. That is the denial of liberty, and leads straight to its overthrow. A society in which men recognize no check upon their freedom soon becomes a society where freedom is the possession of only a savage few; as we have learned to our sorrow.

What, then, is the spirit of liberty? I cannot define it; I can only tell you my own faith. The spirit of liberty is the spirit which is not too sure that it is right; the spirit of liberty is the spirit which seeks to understand the minds of other men and women; the spirit of liberty is the spirit which weights their interests alongside its own without bias; the spirit of liberty remembers that not even a sparrow falls to earth unheeded.

SUSAN B. ANTHONY

FROM

Is it a Crime for a Citizen of the United States to Vote?

1873

IT was we, the people; not we, the white male citizens; nor yet we, the male citizens; but we, the whole people, who formed the Union.

MARTIN LUTHER KING JR.

FROM HIS

Address at the March on Washington

August 28, 1963

I SAY to you today, my friends, that in spite of the difficulties and frustrations of the moment I still have a dream. It is a dream deeply rooted in the American dream. I have a dream that one day this nation will rise up and live out the true meaning of its creed: "We hold these truths to be self-evident; that all men are created equal."

I have a dream that one day on the red hills of Georgia the sons of former slaves and the sons of former slaveowners will be able to sit down together at the table of brotherhood.

I have a dream that one day even the state of Mississippi, a desert state sweltering with the heart of injustice and oppression, will be transformed into an oasis of freedom and justice.

I have a dream that my four little children will one day live in a nation where they will not be judged by the color of their skin but by the content of their character.

I have a dream today.

I have a dream that one day the state of Alabama, whose governor's lips are presently dripping with the words of interposition and nullification, will be transformed into a situation where little black boys and black girls will be able to join hands with little white boys and girls and walk together as sisters and brothers.

I have a dream today.

I have a dream that one day every valley shall be exalted, every hill and mountain shall be made low, the rough places will be made plain, and the crooked places will be made straight, and the glory of the Lord shall be revealed, and all flesh shall see it together....

This will be the day when all of God's children will be able to sing with new meaning, "My country 'tis of thee, sweet land of liberty, of thee I sing. Land where my father died, land of the Pilgrims' pride, from every mountainside, let freedom ring."

And when this happens, when we allow freedom to ring, when we let it ring from every village and every hamlet, from every state and every city, we will be able to speed up that day when *all* of God's children, black men and white men, Jews and Gentiles, Protestants and Catholics, will be able to join hands and sing in the words of the old Negro spiritual:

Free at last! Free at last!

Thank God Almighty, we are free at last!

True American
Patriotism

A SPEECH TO AMERICA

FRIENDS, FELLOW AMERICANS,

I am a progressive. And I am a patriot.

There are many who think these two things don't go together. They say that true progressives don't believe in patriotism and that true patriots don't believe in progressivism.

And I am here today to say that they are dead wrong.

Now, these skeptics—these folks who say a progressive patriot is like a fish with wings—come from both the right and the left.

There are many conservatives today who believe the very word "patriot" means not-liberal. In their minds, liberalism is a school of self-hating and self-blaming. In their minds, liberals are weak and ineffectual, too slow to see our enemies, domestic and foreign, and too quick to forgive those enemies. In their minds, liberals know only what is wrong with America and take for granted all that is right.

Never mind that these conservative critics play fast and loose with the truth and sell slander like a brand. The bad news is, they are good at what they do. The worse news is that this phony cartoon image of liberalism has become ingrained in the popular imagination.

And the tragic news is that there are liberals who unwittingly play right into it.

For today, there are too many liberals who have an allergic, reflexive reaction against the very idea of patriotism. In their minds, to be a patriot means to love war or to be an imperialist bully or to be a closed-minded neocon. In their minds, love of country blots out the problems in other countries or the problems that cross national borders. In their minds, conservatives are brutes and simpletons who don't see all the nuance of the world.

And so, over the last four decades of American politics, the right has grabbed the turf of patriotism. But that's because the left abandoned it. The right didn't just steal patriotism; the left left it unprotected.

For years, from Vietnam through the Carter years, from Reagan to the end of the Cold War, from 9/11 to the war in Iraq, a song has been playing over and over in our politics. That song says the right loves America, and the left looks down on it. It says conservatives are proud to wave the flag and proclaim America to be the best, and liberals, embarrassed by the whole chest-thumping spectacle, complain about America's errors.

And gradually, over the course of these decades, too many average Americans have learned this song. They have decided they fundamentally can't trust liberals. Voters may repudiate overreaching conservatives. But they're not running to embrace uncertain liberals.

I'm here today to talk about a new vision of patriot-ism, one that breaks this paradigm. My aim isn't just to defend liberals—my liberal friends will come in for plenty of criticism, and I am perfectly willing to admit where conservatives have gotten it right. The spirit of this new patriotism is, like the oldest forms of American patriotism, above faction and party.

True American patriotism belongs neither to liber-als nor conservatives. It does not belong to people who think of electoral or partisan advantage first. True American patriotism belongs to us, the com-mon sense people who have grown tired of the left–right tracks of ideologues and ideology. It belongs to common sense people who are willing to sacrifice to create something better for their children, who are yearning to connect to something larger than them-selves. These people may not know what is ideologi-cally correct. They simply know what makes sense and what works.

For too long, ideologues, both liberals and conserva-tives, have taken these people too much for granted. Liberals have too often forgotten what values and purpose mean. Conservatives have too often forgotten that their values are not the only values, nor their purpose the only purpose.

Today it is time for us to speak directly to both liberals and conservatives, and to declare that a new, patriotic path—grounded in common sense, guided by traditional virtues, and focused on progress—is the path of our nation's future. It is time for those of us who love our country, and cannot abide another election of ideology, to declare a new politics of purpose: a renewed American patriotism.

We have grown frustrated by those on the right who call dissent unpatriotic and by those on the left who think dissent is the only measure of their patriotism. One side says, "If you don't like it, leave it." The other side says, "I'll stay if I like it." Neither side commits to the actual work of improving our country. The conservatives who say, "My country, right or wrong," are like permissive parents spoiling a bad child. The liberals who say, "My country, only if right," are like domineering, manipulative parents withholding their love to get the desired behavior. But true love of country is tough love—and it's unconditional love.

As Senator Carl Schurz stated over a century ago, true patriotism means, "Our country—*when right to be kept right; when wrong to be put right.*"

The problem is too few leaders lead like that today. We are tired of politicians who think that leadership is telling us what we want to hear and that the means of election are the ends of politics. We are sick of pandering promises—but hungry for leaders who will challenge us. We are ashamed of how our politics today abuses love of country—but we are unabashed about expressing what is truly great about America.

To the liberals of this nation: You are the proud inheritors of a great tradition. It is no overstatement to say that America would not be America without you and liberals before you.

In each generation, our nation's highest ideals have been put to the test by people like you: people who held up an unflattering mirror to a complacent society; who insisted that what seemed to be the natural order of things was simply a game unfairly rigged; people who demanded that the nation live up, at

long last, to the intent and promises of our founders and Constitution. Freedom, equality, opportunity, justice. Promises long denied and deferred for
so many people at so many times in our history—
denied and deferred, that is, until someone finally
said, "This is not good enough. This is not right. This
is not American."

And yet liberal politics, like any kind of politics, can
get stuck in its own ways. For several decades now
the liberal base of the electorate has slowly eroded.
Too much liberal energy has gone into defending
the aging edifice of the New Deal and the Great
Society. Too little energy has gone into imagining
a New New Deal, and making it matter. Too many
liberals have insisted on rights without responsi-
bilities. Too few have tried to understand what has
driven so many Americans to the other side.

What many liberals have forgotten during this time
is the value of purpose and the language of patriotism.

What does purpose mean? It means the deepest
desire for our short lives to mean something.

Americans are raised to believe in the future, that

the future will be better, and that we have it in our own power to make things better. And because we are raised to believe these things, to believe in them even when the cruel hard facts of our own lives speak against belief—because of this we want all the more to find in our politics a validation of this belief.

We want our leaders to believe as we do, that there is a point to all this striving—that life adds up, that the struggle matters and the sacrifice counts. And this is where some liberals have fallen down on the job. You have spoken of programs. You have spoken of process. You have spoken of rights. But you have not in a very long time spoken of your values, of human needs and fears and wants and dreams. And without this, you do not earn the trust of people who want to be heard and truly recognized, who want their lives to make sense and matter—and who want this at least as much as they want this entitlement or that program.

You have told us about great global forces of change. You have told us that such forces can reduce and destabilize our lives and our prospects. But you have not in a very long time spoken of how your ideas will make us any more capable of navigating the chaos of our times. And without that, you simply sound like those who can't *do*, and therefore you don't matter to most Americans.

You have taught us the value of sensitivity to others, and diversity of perspective. This is to the good. But you have not in a long time made Americans feel that beneath all this compassion and tolerance, you have a rock-ribbed sense of right and wrong, true and false, reward and punishment. And without that, you can't earn the full confidence of a people in search of moral leadership.

To speak a language of purpose is to say, "The life that matters is a life devoted to developing our fullest God-given potential. The purpose of our days is to create a legacy that lasts *beyond* our days. And the purpose of our politics must be to arm every American with a fair shot to build the best life possible for themselves and their families."

To speak a language of purpose is not to take code words like "moral values" and "faith" and transplant them into otherwise unchanged liberal wish lists. That is a cynical, tactical and ultimately useless exercise.

To speak a language of purpose is to return to first principles and to be able to answer, in plain English, the plain questions of Why? Why should we chip in to help someone else? Why should we defer gratification? Why should we care about the long term? Why should we trust anyone who seems to be limiting our ability to do what we want? And why should we listen to you at all?

Liberalism has too often come to stand for an indulgent morality: a morality of benefits without work, achievement without sacrifice, choices without consequences. Is this a fair caricature? No. But it does describe what millions of Americans feel in their gut about liberalism. About *you*.

You have told us about the unfair plight of those at the bottom. And that plight *is*, in many ways, unfair. But in focusing so much on those at the bottom, and talking mainly about what's been done to them rather than what they can do for themselves, you have left a broad middle of the populace feeling like liberalism is neither about them nor for them.

Liberals have told us much about what is wrong with America and all that remains broken. To be sure, a great deal *is* wrong with America. And to be sure, there can be no progress without a candid assessment of our failings. But over time, too many liberals have forgotten how to speak—from the heart—of the greatness of this nation, the deep reservoir of resilience and earnestness and endurance and optimism that will enable us to overcome anything.

Instead, you have allowed a group of people with a narrow view of what it means to be American to claim for themselves the title "True American." You have allowed your counterparts on the right to claim American as their own.

This is a colossal failure—of vision, of heart, of guts and of brains. And this is why liberals need to steep themselves again in the traditions of patriotism.

To do this does not mean recasting patriotism away from guns and flags. It means grabbing those guns and flags. It means saying that the guns that cleared a path on the beaches of Normandy, the flags that were finally planted in the ash of Iwo Jima, were brought to bear in the service of something greater than "Every man for himself." Something higher than "Chase the almighty dollar." Something deeper than "Settle for whatever freedom is granted to you."

True, traditional American patriotism means saying that this is a nation worth loving—openly, unabashedly, furiously—and that every sacrifice past and present can be made worthwhile only—only—by committing ourselves to a program of more progress, more opportunity, for more of our countrymen and women. It means taking hold of what works and shedding what holds us back.

Because otherwise, what was it all for?

Otherwise, why should America hold itself distinct from the nations of Europe or Asia or all points between? What should make us special, make our common heritage worth loving, *except* the idea that in this country we move *humanity* forward? Progress. This is the country where everyone gets to rewrite their own story and invent their own future. This is the country where newcomers who had never been allowed to try or to be, because of what they were or were not, now get the chance to create and to become. Do they often fail? Yes. Do many fall short of the dream? Yes. But are they grateful to be in a place where there is a chance? Yes—and so it should be in our feelings toward this country. We fail. We falter. And the root of our greatness is that we get up. And then succeed.

This is the country of progress. To love progress is to love America. And if you truly love America, liberals, if you are truly willing to put yourself on the line for your nation, then now more than ever you must infuse every aspect of your program with a new sense of purpose: national purpose, personal purpose, each reinforcing the other. And you must describe that purpose in terms that make us proud: not only to be Americans, but to be Americans alongside *you*.

Now, to my conservative friends:

For the past half century, you also have been right about a lot: about the unintended negative consequences of well-meaning social programs; about the power of liberty to cause great walls of tyranny to tumble; about the need to lead in the world with clarity of purpose.

You've been right that this nation was founded not only on high-minded ideals but on a bedrock of virtue, of old-fashioned values like responsibility and discipline and respect for tradition. And you've been right to worry that in many quarters, those values are eroding.

But here is where so many of you have been wrong: You've been wrong to assume that the market is always right.

You've been wrong to assert that what you fear must be evil.

You've been wrong to leave so many disenfranchised and unfavored people on the sidelines of public life, and off the roster of our national team.

And you've been wrong to assert that citizens working together to solve shared problems—in a word, government—is itself the problem.

There are too many people calling themselves

conservative today who are preaching selfishness, narrowness, hatefulness and fear; who have replaced the word of God with the hand of the market. That is not you. That is not what you want to protect and preserve. You are a conservative for good reasons: because there is no substitute for tradition and its timeless truths. Because if you cut the cord to our past, then it gets awfully hard to make sense of the present or the future. And yet the market, and the market ethic of naked selfishness, does cut that cord every day.

So I say to conservatives, isn't the market that so many of you worship the very thing that erodes your sense of standards and tradition?

You believe in freedom. And so you may believe that any government infringement upon your pursuit of happiness is wrong. But you are smart enough to know just what your pursuit of happiness would be like without roads. Without schools. Without courts to punish criminals. Without cops to catch them. Without clean water. Without someone to ensure your bank deposits or your bodily health. You know well that any freedom worth having is never free.

So I say to conservatives, if you love your country, will you put your money where your mouth is? Are you willing to pay a price for freedom?

As a conservative, you believe in responsibility. And so you believe, for instance, that a welfare recipient must value work and the idea of earning one's way in the world. But this notion of responsibility should extend to the rich as well, to the recipients of gigantic tax breaks and tailor-made tax loopholes. And it should extend as well to the responsibility our *society* has to those who work hard and play by the rules but who live in fear that an illness or a layoff will send their families into free-fall.

So I ask conservatives, why should wealthy deadbeats upset you any less than poor ones? Whom are you willing to punish for not pulling their weight? And what are you willing to do for working Americans who *do* pull their weight and still struggle to make ends meet?

As a conservative, you believe in spending wisely. And so you believe, for instance, that when a politician proposes new taxes for some new program, the proper response is "not one more penny for *them.*" But do you know which of the pennies are for you? Is it the pennies that pay for your home mortgage interest deduction? The pennies that pay for your parents' Medicare drug benefit? The pennies that subsidize college tuition?

What are you willing to call investment in America?

As a conservative, you believe in a natural order of things. But some part of you knows that not everyone rich has earned it and not everyone poor deserves it. Somewhere, you recognize that deserts are not always just. You know in your heart that a 25-year-old Wall Street bond trader earning tens of millions per year is not in fact worth several hundred times more to America than a 55-year-old schoolteacher earning tens of thousands.

What are you willing to do to correct this unnatural imbalance?

As a conservative, you believe in sacrifice. And so you believe, for instance, that those who serve in our armed forces should be honored for their willingness to sacrifice. Indeed they should. But what about the rest of us? How is it that we are in a "war on terror" and have not been asked to do anything more than shop? We have learned in this age of outsourcing to outsource sacrifice itself.

What are you willing to sacrifice for the good of the country?

Finally, as a conservative, you believe in honesty. And for years you've loved firebrands of the right who promise to tell it like it is—to cut through political correctness and get down to the facts. But now, as this administration buries the facts on so many fronts—about the reason for going to Iraq, but also about the abuses of the so-called Patriot Act, about the scope of the failure of Katrina, about the political thuggery of the Justice Department—now you realize it's not the left that is engaged in disinformation and bad faith politics.

So are you willing to call it like it is?

You know that conservatism was never meant to be blind orthodoxy. You know this country well enough to see that "my way or the highway" is exactly what the Founders fled.

The conservative's blessing is that he is always rooted to the past. The conservative's curse is that the future is unrelenting. It's a simple practical question: how can we face our tomorrows with all the assembled might and wisdom of our yesterdays? This, my conservative friends, should be the true measure of our patriotism: whether, for a new generation, we can make the liberty our forefathers created worth living for.

These are the faults of the liberal path and the conservative path. And here is the alternative. A real choice.

The real choice is a new American patriotism.

I mean a patriotism that is more practical than ideological, focusing on the good of the country more than the self-interest of the individual. I mean a patriotism that recognizes that the true power of America comes not from our economic output or military might but from our values and our never-ending effort to live up to our founding ideals. I mean a patriotism that appeals to that desire in each of us to be part of something larger than ourselves.

So I reject ideologues of every stripe who insist that the purity of their cause matters more than the world as it is. I reject those who cloak their selfishness behind the fancy justifications of natural law or the market's hidden hand. I reject those who tell us that greed is good and righteous. I reject those who expect something for nothing, regardless of their willingness to earn, learn and sacrifice. I reject those who think that getting it now is the American way.

There is another American way, as old as America itself. Long before the revolution, the very first settlers of this land came rooted in a tradition of shared sacrifice and common cause. This land became a great nation because countless millions wanted to better themselves—but they all knew that to better yourself meant to better your neighbor, and to better all your children. And with each passing generation, from settlement to colony to state to union, they laid down an American habit: relentless progress and possibility through deep adherence to old-fashioned virtues.

It is time to revive this American way.

We are all responsible for this. We all have to make the small choices that add up to big change. We all have to send out ripples of hope with our own actions as individual citizens. But there's another way we are all responsible, and that is defined by the kind of leaders we all demand.

The best and worst thing about living in a democracy is that it always gives us the leaders we deserve. That's why if we want great leaders, we must demand great citizenship of ourselves. And we must be explicit about the quality and character of leadership we want and prefer.

So let's agree that we patriots want leaders who are first and foremost honest with us. And the essence of this brutal honesty is that they ask us to be patriots, and to put America first, to sacrifice for the common good. Their message is never one of instant gratification, one that encourages us to live easier, work less, give less or share less. Their message is never one which encourages selfishness or self-indulgence.

Honest people know that the road to success and virtue always involves shared sacrifice, hard work and gratification postponed. Telling people otherwise isn't leadership, it is pandering. We've had enough of that.

America deserves leaders who insist that politics isn't about the promotion and protection of self-interest, it should be about promoting the interest of all Americans.

America deserves leaders who remind us that our worth as citizens is a consequence of our contribution to community and that those who have benefited most owe the greatest debt of gratitude and service.

America deserves leaders who help us understand one another, not drive us apart.

America deserves leaders who encourage us to conserve resources, not to exploit them, and know that wasting less is more patriotic than buying more.

We want leaders who inspire us with their actions as well as words and who embody the best of American honesty, hard work, independence, compassion and patriotism.

Our first duty as citizens is to be honest with ourselves and to distrust those who preach only what we want to hear; who tell us that America will be better off if we treat taxation as confiscation; if our resources are more deeply exploited; if our public infrastructure and institutions more neglected; if our children are made to pay later for today's profligate spending; if our own views and faiths are used to suppress the views and faiths of others.

We know, in our hearts, that such a path leads to slow-motion ruin.

Now we have to imagine a better path.

Imagine an elected leader unafraid to challenge us, who pushes us, by word and deed, to curb our unhealthiest national habits and reinforce our best ones. Picture it: a politician who truly puts country above party or self—and is rewarded for it by the voters.

Imagine a country where being an active citizen brings us as much spiritual and emotional fulfillment as being a parent or grandparent. Picture it: an impassioned Great Awakening that sends us and all our neighbors into a revival of civic participation— in our clubs, churches and communities.

Imagine a time when all Americans truly do heed John Kennedy's call to "ask what you can do for your country."

Picture it: young people who want to serve the community not because it looks good on a college application but because it flows from the values and ethics their parents and teachers have imbued them with.

Imagine a society where all of us, powerful or not, find it offensive when great gaps open up between the richest and the poorest. Picture it: Americans of every income bracket supporting policies that will pull up those in the brackets below.

Imagine a vital economy that draws on the full talents and potential of every American worker. Picture it: the kind of mobilization of human capital that we saw in World War II, but this time, leaving no groups out in the cold.

Imagine a new social contract in which employers see workers as whole human beings and not unit labor costs, and in which workers feel like creators of the future rather than mere consumers of it. Picture it: a new American ethic that says the economy exists to serve *us,* not vice versa.

Imagine the day when America is the object of worldwide admiration, not only because we cut back on greenhouse gas emissions dramatically but also because we did so by launching an innovative green economy. Picture it: other nations, large and small, racing to imitate America—and the world being better off for it.

Imagine the pride our children and their children will take in us, if we make the hard decisions today to restore American credibility around the world and to strengthen the social fabric at home. Picture it: history books that describe these times—our moment—as the "Pivot Generation," the era when things could have gone bad and instead turned around, enduringly, for the good.

We are Americans. By definition, we believe in something better. We can imagine it. Now we must demand it. And when we do, we will set this country firmly on the path to progress.

That, my friends, is the *true* meaning of patriotism.

JANE ADDAMS

FROM ·

Newer Ideals of Peace

Published in 1907

UNLESS our conception of patriotism is progressive,
it cannot hope to embody the real affection and the real
interest of the nation.

Let America Be America Again

July 1936

O, let America be America again—
The land that never has been yet—
And yet must be—
The land where every man is free.
The land that's mine—
The poor man's, Indian's, Negro's, ME—
Who made America,
Whose sweat and blood, whose faith and pain,
Whose hand at the foundry, whose plow in the rain,
Must bring back our mighty dream again.

O, yes,
I say it plain,
America never was America to me,
And yet I swear this oath—
America will be!
An ever-living seed,
Its dream
Lies deep in the heart of me.

JOHN F. KENNEDY

FROM HIS

Inaugural Address

January 20, 1961

We observe today not a victory of party, but a celebration
of freedom—symbolizing an end, as well as a beginning—
signifying renewal, as well as change. For I have sworn before
you and Almighty God the same solemn oath our forebears
prescribed nearly a century and three quarters ago.

The world is very different now. For man holds in his
mortal hands the power to abolish all forms of human
poverty and all forms of human life. And yet the same
revolutionary beliefs for which our forebears fought are still
at issue around the globe—the belief that the rights of man
come not from the generosity of the state, but from the hand
of God.

We dare not forget today that we are the heirs of that first
revolution. Let the word go forth from this time and place,
to friend and foe alike, that the torch has been passed to
a new generation of Americans—born in this century,

tempered by war, disciplined by a hard and bitter peace, proud of our ancient heritage—and unwilling to witness or permit the slow undoing of those human rights to which this Nation has always been committed, and to which we are committed today at home and around the world....

In your hands, my fellow citizens, more than in mine, will rest the final success or failure of our course. Since this country was founded, each generation of Americans has been summoned to give testimony to its national loyalty. The graves of young Americans who answered the call to service surround the globe.

Now the trumpet summons us again—not as a call to bear arms, though arms we need; not as a call to battle, though embattled we are—but a call to bear the burden of a long twilight struggle, year in and year out, "rejoicing in hope, patient in tribulation"—a struggle against the common enemies of man: tyranny, poverty, disease, and war itself.

Can we forge against these enemies a grand and global alliance, North and South, East and West, that can assure a more fruitful life for all mankind? Will you join in that historic effort?

In the long history of the world, only a few generations have been granted the role of defending freedom in its hour of maximum danger. I do not shrink from this responsibility— I welcome it. I do not believe that any of us would exchange places with any other people or any other generation. The energy, the faith, the devotion which we bring to this endeavor will light our country and all who serve it—and the glow from that fire can truly light the world.

And so, my fellow Americans: ask not what your country can do for you—ask what you can do for your country.

My fellow citizens of the world: ask not what America will do for you, but what together we can do for the freedom of man.

Finally, whether you are citizens of America or citizens of the world, ask of us the same high standards of strength and sacrifice which we ask of you. With a good conscience our only sure reward, with history the final judge of our deeds, let us go forth to lead the land we love, asking His blessing and His help, but knowing that here on earth God's work must truly be our own.

Ask
What *You* Can Do

OUR OBJECT IN THIS PAMPHLET has been to reclaim patriotism and connect it back to its original pragmatic and progressive roots. Our definition of patriotism transcends self, rejects selfish values and exalts service, responsibility, contribution and commitment.

Our larger goal is to ignite a national conversation about patriotism and *public* morality. The title of this work—"True Patriot"—is purposely provocative and judgmental. It reflects our view that we are *not* all equal: some Americans more fully embody the values and the promise of American life than others.

But this conversation won't happen unless *you* carry it forward. So, to our political leaders: Ask yourself why you got into this business. Know your own values and principles. State them to us. Lead with them. Engage us in arguments about the *why* of politics—then, and only then, tell us about the how. We don't want the plumbing; we want the architecture.

To our citizen readers: Go to a town meeting or call your political leaders—but instead of pleading this cause or that, demand that your leaders articulate their first principles. Question them on their operating values, and their public morality, and judge them: by whether they live up to their values, and by whether their values live up to our country.

These steps may seem simple and naïve. They are. And they are the only way we will cut through all the cynical posturing, coded language and kabuki gestures that constitute modern politics. We have offered up *our* best articulation of what we think patriotism means. We hope you will accept these ideas. But if you do not, we invite you—indeed, challenge you—to use this document as grist for debate and discussion and to spell out your own ideas.

So we leave you now with several questions that we hope can stimulate reflection and prompt you to action. Ask yourself these questions. Ask all those around you. Listen to the responses. Repeat the cycle. And then share *your* vision with other Americans.

That is how we will make our country all it can truly be.

- What is *your* moral code? What are your 10 guiding principles?

- What does patriotism mean to you? What does it mean to your friends and family?

- What three acts can you take—at home, at work, at worship or in civic life—to demonstrate stewardship, contribution over consumption, mutual obligation or any of the other tenets of true American patriotism? What ripples do those acts create?

- Which public leaders best exemplify the spirit of true American patriotism? What actions will you take to encourage those leaders? What actions will you take to become one of those leaders?

- What do you want Americans a century from now to be most proud of when they look back at the choices our generation made?

———

We invite you to join us at our website, *truepat.org*, to share your ideas, post your writings, challenge ours and spark more conversation.

E pluribus unum

From many, one

ABOUT THE AUTHORS

ERIC LIU is an author and educator based in Seattle. He served as a speechwriter and a senior domestic policy adviser to President Bill Clinton.

NICK HANAUER is a Seattle-based entrepreneur and venture capitalist. He is active in many progressive civic and philanthropic organizations and causes.

IMAGE CREDITS